AMAZON ANIMALS

A COLORING BOOK WITH A HIDDEN PICTURE TWIST

JAN SOVAK

DOVER PUBLICATIONS, INC.
MINEOLA, NEW YORK

This coloring book features twenty-eight adventure-filled illustrations of wildlife in the Amazon. The realistic images depict everything from anacondas and jaguars to toucans and tarantulas! A hidden picture component running through the entire book makes it even more interesting. Answers are included, and the illustrations are printed on one side of a perforated page for easy removal and display.

Bibliographical Note

Amazon Animals: A Coloring Book with a Hidden Picture Twist, first published by Dover Publications, Inc., in 2015, contains some of the artwork from *Lost in the Amazon Hidden Pictures,* originally published by Dover in 2011.

International Standard Book Number

ISBN-13: 978-0-486-79899-8
ISBN-10: 0-486-79899-2

Manufactured in the United States by LSC Communications
79899204   2018
www.doverpublications.com

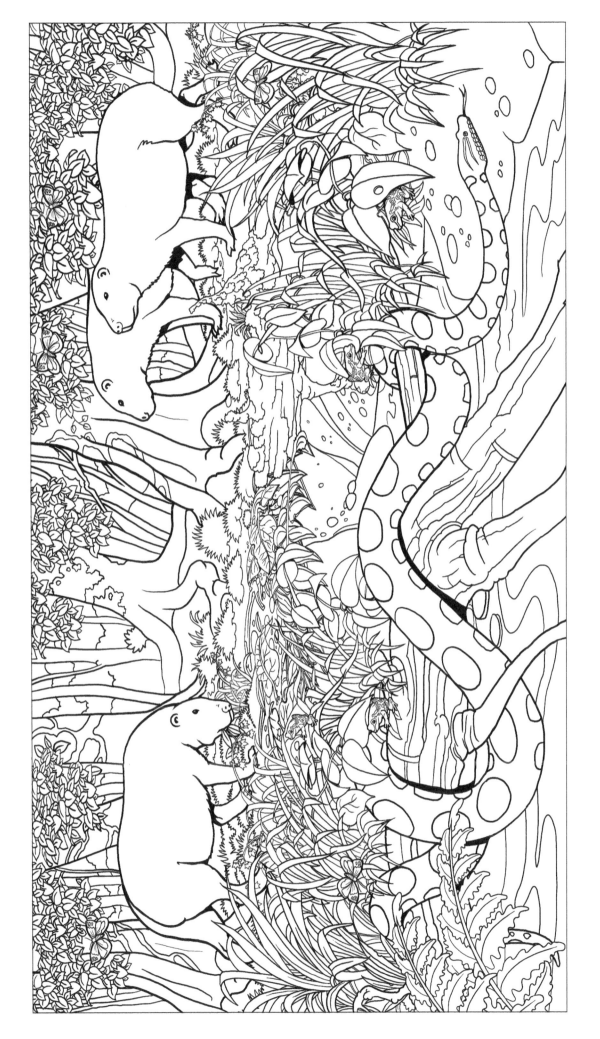

SOLUTIONS

page 1
Lycid Beetles (4)

page 2
Jaguar, Butterflies (7)

page 3
Jungle Snails (4)

page 4
Viper Snake, Long-bill Birds (3)

page 5
Mice (7)

page 6
Beetles (4), Golden Flowers (8)

page 7
Frogs (4), Butterflies (5)

page 8
Fish (5), Water Snails (6)

page 9
Lizards (3), Beetles (7)

page 10
Snakes (2)

page 11
Fish (5), Snails (6)

page 12
Lizards (3), Butterflies (5)

page 13
Orchid Flowers (6)

page 14
Blue Flowers (3),
Palm Fruit Grapes (4)

page 15
Margay, Giant Wasps (3)

page 16
Aphids (3), Flies (3)

page 17
Beetles (5)

page 18
Butterflies (13),
Hummingbirds (13)

page 19
Turtles (2), Fish (9)

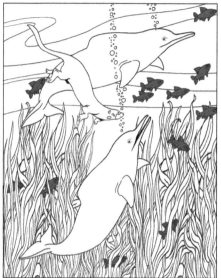

page 20
Fish (12)

page 21
Eggs (19)

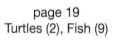

page 22
Frogs (5)

page 23
Ants (6)

page 24
Snake

page 25
Butterflies (4)

page 26
Giant Grasshoppers (3), Bugs (3)

page 27
Woodpeckers (3), Moths (3)

page 28
Fish (12)